For:

_____

From:

_____

Date:

_____

Dedicated to my dear friend, Michelle Rapkin, who was responsible for editing and publishing my first book, *A Travel Guide to Heaven.*

– Anthony DeStefano

This is dedicated to my nieces Melanie and Mariel.

– Erwin Madrid

A Travel Guide to Heaven FOR KIDS

Text copyright © 2013 by Anthony DeStefano
Artwork copyright © 2013 by Erwin Madrid

Published by Harvest House Publishers
Eugene, Oregon 97402
www.harvesthousepublishers.com

ISBN 978-0-7369-5509-6

For more information about Anthony DeStefano, please visit his website
www.anthonydestefano.com.

All works of art in this book are copyrighted by Erwin Madrid and may not be
reproduced without the artist's permission. For information regarding art prints
featured in this book, please contact: erwinmadrid.com.

Design and production by Mary pat Design, Westport, Connecticut

Printed in China
13 14 15 16 17 18 19 20 21 / LP / 10 9 8 7 6 5 4 3 2 1

A Travel Guide to Heaven

FOR KIDS

Anthony DeStefano

Illustrated by Erwin Madrid

HARVEST HOUSE PUBLISHERS
EUGENE, OREGON

"Mom, where do people go when they die?" Joey asked one day.

"They go to heaven to be with Jesus," his mother answered.

"And are they happy in heaven?"

"They're very happy, Joey. Heaven is a very special place."

Joey went into his room and lay down on his bed. He was sad that people and animals had to die. He didn't understand why. He stared up at the ceiling, thinking for a long time. Soon it was dark out and time to go to sleep, but Joey couldn't stop thinking about heaven. *I wonder what heaven is really like,* Joey thought. *I wish I knew.*

Soon Joey drifted off to sleep and started to dream.
Suddenly he heard a tapping at the window.

"Psst!" came a whisper.

"Who's that?" Joey said.

"Psst. Over here."

4

When Joey looked at the window, he saw a face staring back at him. At first it looked like a little girl. But it couldn't be. This little girl had wings!

"Who are you?" asked Joey.

"My name is Gabby," said the girl, "and I'm your guardian angel."

"My guardian angel?" Joey asked in disbelief.

"Sure. Everyone has a guardian angel. Our job is to watch over people and protect them. Only you can't usually see us. We're invisible."

"If you're invisible, then how can I see you now?" asked Joey.

"Well, I'm here for a special reason. I know that you've been wondering a lot about heaven lately, and I'm here to take you on a little tour. Would you like to visit heaven and see it for yourself?"

"Can you really take me to heaven?" Joey asked. "How?"

"It's easy," answered Gabby. "I can have you there and back before it's time for you to go to school tomorrow."

"But I can't fly," said Joey.

"No problem at all," said Gabby, who suddenly pulled from out of nowhere a very odd-looking suitcase. The suitcase was old and battered, as if it had traveled to many places, but the most incredible thing about it was that it had wings—just like Gabby.

The little angel opened her odd-looking suitcase and pulled out a beautiful pin with the word "VISITOR" written on it in shiny gold letters. She handed it to Joey.

"Here. Put this on," said Gabby. "This visitor's pass will allow you to get into heaven and then leave when we're finished with our tour. All you have to do is hop onto my suitcase and buckle up. Hold on tight and count to ten. By the time you're done, we'll be there."

"I'm ready to go," Joey said fearlessly and jumped onto the suitcase.

"One, two, three, four, five, six, seven, eight, nine," he counted as he and Gabby flew over the trees and up through the clouds. By the time Joey reached ten, he could see a magnificent golden gate made of sparkling jewels and shiny white pearls coming into view.

"That's heaven's gate," said Gabby.

Everything looked so bright, colorful, and happy. Joey could hear music everywhere. Beyond the jeweled gates, crowds of people were standing together. They were all smiling and laughing. Joey looked to Gabby to explain what the people were doing.

"They're celebrating," Gabby said. "That's what happens when people die and go to heaven. They're greeted with love by all their friends and family. Grandpas, grandmas, mothers, fathers, sons, and daughters—everyone is here! They know that they will never again be separated, never again be sick, never again be sad or cry—and they will be able to live here together in heaven forever and ever."

Flying high over the landscape, Joey was in awe. Everything was so beautiful. Mountains, rivers, waterfalls, rainbows, and trees were everywhere. Never before had Joey seen such colors: the bluest blues, the reddest reds, and the greenest greens.

And there were cities too, fabulous sparkling cities with golden streets and tall buildings that were bright, shiny, and new. Joey looked down and saw a big amusement park right below them. There were roller coasters, Ferris wheels, bumper cars, carousels, and even Joey's favorite—cotton candy! Everywhere he looked, people were having fun.

"I'd like to go on a ride," Joey said.

"If you *really* want to go for a ride, follow me," said Gabby, who pointed to the sky and started flying upward.

"Okay," said Joey, "I'm right behind you."

ZOOM! They both flew up, over the tops of the
buildings, through the clouds, past the rainbows,
and into outer space. In seconds they were flying
alongside planets and stars. "All this is part of
heaven," Gabby said. "Anyone who lives here can
explore the entire galaxy."

Diving downward again, Joey and Gabby flew back through the clouds. Joey spotted a herd of giraffes drinking from a small lake. "Can we go down there so I can see them better?" he asked.

Once they were on the ground, Joey could see animals of all kinds—lions, lambs, tigers, horses, zebras, elephants, peacocks, bunnies, and birds. And there were hundreds of cats and dogs playing with each other. They all seemed to be having the best time. "Don't the animals ever fight with each other?" Joey asked.

"No. They never fight. They all get along. Everyone in heaven gets along. That's one of the very best things about living here."

"Look up!" Gabby said suddenly. Above the trees Joey could see the head of a giant brontosaurus looking down at them.

"Are there dinosaurs here too?" Joey asked excitedly.

"Of course," replied Gabby. "Every kind of animal that ever lived on the Earth is here."

For a second Joey was scared. But when the dinosaur smiled at him, he felt safe. The friendly dinosaur stretched his long neck down until Joey was able to pet his head. After a moment the dinosaur turned his massive body around and left, causing the ground to shake as he walked and leaving huge footprints behind him.

"I would love to take a ride on his back," said Joey.

"One day you will," said Gabby, "but right now it's time to show you the best part of heaven."

23

Once again they were flying through the air. Gabby pointed to a bright light in the distance and headed toward it. They landed on the ground not far from a rolling green hill. Joey could see the light coming from just beyond the top of the hill. Colorful rays of yellow and orange and gold were streaming from the light in all directions. Gabby and Joey walked toward it.

Joey stopped and looked in amazement. "I've never seen anything so beautiful in my whole life," he said.

"That's where God lives," Gabby said. "One day when you live here, you'll be able to go over the hill and meet Him face-to-face."

"What's God like?" Joey asked. "He must be incredible."

"Oh, He is," Gabby said. "He created all this. He created heaven so that all of us who love Him could be happy. And this is His home, Joey. When people die, they come to live here. They leave their home on Earth, and they come to live in God's home—heaven!"

"I see," said Joey. "And everyone here is happy forever."

"That's right. But it's getting late now," Gabby said, looking at her watch. "It's time to take you back to your house."

Joey reluctantly hopped back onto the suitcase, and the two of them took off. As they flew over the big jeweled gate once again, Joey turned his head back for one last look at heaven. He smiled brightly.

When they got back to Joey's house, it was morning and almost time for Joey to go to school.

"Thank you very much, Gabby," said Joey. "Heaven is the most wonderful place I've ever been to. I'm so glad you took me there."

"You're very welcome," said Gabby. "I have to go now, but remember even though you won't be able to see me anymore, I'll always be here, very close by, watching over you. That's my job!"

And with that, the little angel disappeared.

Just then Joey heard a knock on the door, and his mother walked into his room. "Good morning, Joey," she said. "It's time for school."

"Okay, Mom, but first I've got to tell you about heaven. You'll never believe it, but I was just there!"

"What are you talking about?" his mother asked, looking at him strangely.

"I just got back from heaven! My guardian angel, Gabby, took me there for a special visit. And heaven is the *greatest* place, Mom!"

Joey's mother looked at her son and smiled. "That was just a dream, honey, a wonderful dream."

"No, Mommy. It really happened. I promise."

Seeing her son so excited and happy, Joey's mother decided not to argue with him. "You can tell me all about it after school," she said. "Meanwhile, hurry up or you'll be late."

As Joey's mother started to make his bed, a small object fell to the floor. She picked it up and saw that it was a beautiful pin with the word "VISITOR" written on it in shiny gold letters. "What's this?" she asked her son.

Joey just smiled at her as he rushed out the door to school.

My Heaven Prayer

Jesus is the King of all,
The young and old,
The big and small.
And heaven is the wondrous place
Where we will see Him face-to-face,
With no more sadness, no more sighing,
No more sickness, no more crying.
Please save me, Lord, and hear this prayer—
I want to live forever there!
Amen.